WHY CAN'T WE JUST GET ALONG?

TERRY WALDEN

authorHOUSE®

AuthorHouse™
1663 Liberty Drive
Bloomington, IN 47403
www.authorhouse.com
Phone: 1 (800) 839-8640

Published by AuthorHouse 04/19/2019

ISBN: 978-1-7283-0890-6 (sc)
ISBN: 978-1-7283-0889-0 (e)

Library of Congress Control Number: 2019904821

H ello. I'm just an ordinary citizen giving his opinion on the politics and problems that the world is facing today. You only hear from the one-sided media and the politicians—or, as I call them, "the rich people." With all that is going on in our country, I thought it would be a nice change for you to hear from someone who is just like you. And before I give you my thoughts and opinions on what I see as today's problems, let me tell you about myself.

My name is Terry. I'm fifty-three years old, and I own and operate a construction business. I've been in business for thirty-two years, and this business sure has had its ups and downs. I come from a family of six. I have two brothers and a sister. My father was a World War II vet and a deputy sheriff. My mother spent more than forty years working at the RCA plant. My parents were Republicans, so guess what I am. My dad passed away in 1987 of heart failure. My mother passed away in 2005, also from heart trouble. As you can imagine, I keep my heart checked. I miss my parents and how families used to be. I think it is important for families to stay close.

My opinions are from my own experience. And based on what I hear from my friends, it seems as though family isn't like it used to be.

Anyway, back to my business. Some of the hard things in running it were taxes, rules, and regulations. Now it seems as though we have a president who is going to help small business because he knows that small businesses are a big part of this county and hire a lot of today's employees.

Mr. Trump's election is why I have decided to write this book. I have not always been happy with who has been president, but the important part for me is not being a Democrat or Republican; I felt it was my duty as an American citizen to support this person and give him the elected chance to prove himself.

For example, I like President Clinton and thought he did a good job with the way he ran this country—and then, we all know what he did with Monica. But again, the one-sided media didn't know what to do or say about this situation. And then you have President Obama. This one I didn't like, and not at all because of his color—I have many black friends. I don't believe he did a good job at all, and he really hurt our military. Although I feel the way I do, I gave him the benefit of the doubt. This is behind us, and I believe we have elected the best president who has ever been elected of all time. Let me give my opinion of this. Mr. Trump speaks his mind as no other president has. He is more like you and me. He isn't a big politician like past presidents, and he wants to make our country good. We have never seen anything like this before. The media and Democrats don't have any idea how to handle Mr. Trump other than to try to destroy him. I don't understand this. It has brought me to write about it, and I have never written about anything in my life.

Why the hell would you all not be happy about having someone elected who wants to make this country great again?

Mr. Trump wants to do this for all of us and not just for the Republicans. All of us—don't you get this? And, remember: he isn't a Washington politician. We all have a chance to once again become alive, and we all should be 100 percent in support of this. I have never watched the news so much in my life, and I can see what is happening. Here is what I see. There are signs up everywhere: "Help Wanted" or

"Now Hiring." I don't ever remember seeing so many places hiring at one time. It now has been one year since Mr. Trump took office, and look at the changes in that little time. The statistics have come out on 2018's holiday shopping, and it is through the roof. I should say the retailers are happy. I'm excited for this county and want to see what Mr. Trump will do for all of us. As an ordinary citizen, this is what I see and hear when I turn on the news. The media is constantly trying to find something wrong with Mr. Trump. Why does the tweeting bother you? It is interesting to know what our president is thinking. When did you ever know before what the president was thinking? He is our leader, and it is nice knowing what he is thinking.

What the media and Democrats can't leave alone is the idea that he cheated in the election. No, we, the Republicans, just finally got enough of us to vote. The majority of votes from the electoral college wins, and that is not cheating. Let me give you an example of why Mr. Trump was elected. I held a little party at my shop, and at this party were friends, family, and employees. I asked all of them, "How many of you are going to vote?" I told all of them that not voting is the problem and is why Obama was elected. I now know that by the end of my speech to them, at least twelve of them had decided to vote, and most of them for the first time in their lives. This is what I believe has happened all over our country. The Republicans finally got out and voted. Now, what I think we need to do is this: all of you who know Democrats need to try and talk some sense into them and tell them we need to back Mr. Trump and stand behind him. It's this simple: give him the chance, and if you don't like what he does, then get your people out to vote. I just can't grasp why you would want to stop someone who wants to make where you live and come from great again.

You know, I have heard the media put this man down because he has many successful businesses—why? We should look up to that! I heard the media say during the debates that Mr. Trump's father gave him a million dollars, so this father must have been successful too. What's wrong with that? He must have put that money into some really good ideas to be where he is today. The media say he doesn't have the experience to be president of the United States. Well, I think he is showing you all that he has what it takes. The real question here is *why can't we just get along?* You will hear me say this a lot throughout this book.

Mr. Trump surprised me during the debates. I thought his knowledge of foreign affairs was pretty good, but who the hell is going to know everything? There were times when the media tried to make him look stupid.

Mr. Trump held his own pretty well throughout this media bash and the debates. For any one of our presidents, it has to be a hard and trying job to run an entire country, and to have to do this and also deal with the media that we have is unbelievable. Our media should be talking about all the good things this president is doing for us, not trying to put him down. It has to make the job even more difficult. Rather than thinking about white or black, we should all just get along. We shouldn't be judged by race. We should be judged by how we treat each other. Can you imagine how great the country would be if we would all get along? I would now like to speak my opinion on several things I see going on in America. Now, remember: I'm just an ordinary citizen and am just giving my opinion.

Let me begin with the black-and-white issues. You first must know I have many friends who are black, and I am not at all prejudiced. I ask myself why is it when you hear of a black person being shot by a white police officer, all of a sudden you see a damn riot start. And in most cases, this person getting shot is a known criminal and has been in trouble many times before. Now, my question is, how many times do you think a black cop has shot a white person? Well, if you just check, you will see my point: you don't see any riots then. My other question is, where are you people when a black person has shot and killed another black person? This happens all the time in our state and, I'm sure, everywhere else. Let me tell you a story. In our state, two black men broke into a local preacher's house to rob the family, and they killed the preacher's wife, who was pregnant. Where were you riot people for this? I don't understand you. Look at Al Sharpton—he has got to be one of the most unbelievable people I've ever seen on TV. And doesn't he owe a lot of taxes? Just saying. My point again is police officers, white or black, have a tough job, and we all should thank them for their service. If you would keep your ass out of trouble, you wouldn't have to deal with them anyway. We all need to get along and obey the laws that we have; our laws are nothing like the laws in other countries. You cannot believe how great it is to be living in the United States.

There are opportunities out there for everyone, and you have to want to be a better person. You don't have to be out here committing crimes. It is what you choose to do. My other point about this is we have plenty of terrible white people out here committing crimes and murder, doing drugs or selling drugs, and stealing. It all needs to stop. If we don't make our laws stronger—and I mean really stronger—this is not going to stop.

In my state, Indiana, we just set a record for the numbers of murders in a year's time in Indianapolis. Already this year, it is averaging one murder every other day. This is what I wake up to every morning while watching the local new channels. This is very serious, and we've got to get a handle on it. The only way, in my opinion, is stronger laws. One crime that I believe is worse than anyone can believe is theft. There is so much theft. I don't believe people understand how bad it is. I am a victim of theft. I had my twenty-four-foot enclosed race trailer sitting in front of my shop. The thief or thieves cut the locks and took off down the road with it. I had the police out, and they told me I was the fifth person to report a trailer theft that week. I have never been so mad in my life. This was mine, and I worked hard for what I have. Then some damned thief comes and takes it from me.

With my business, I get calls to come fix doors or windows in homes or businesses that have been broken into. At the last one I fixed, the police were there, and I asked them what is going to happen with this problem. The officer said he didn't know. He said they catch them and put them in jail, but the courts let them right back out. This is the problem, and our laws need to be changed. I looked at other countries about the theft problem, and some cut the thieves' hands off so they can't steal again. We have to do something different to stop these thieves. I wish I had the time and money to lead the way to get something done about this. There is nothing that makes me madder than a damned thief. When we throw these people in jail, we have to stop worrying about whether they are fed well, whether they have TV, whether it is too warm or too cold for them, and whether they slept well. This has to stop. Do you think they were worried when they were stealing your belongings? Hell, no.

I'm serious when I say this is a very bad problem. I know because I have several friends who are police officers, and they tell me how bad the theft problem is. This is what I think we should do. When a person decides to steal, on the first offense, give him thirty days in jail with bread and water only. Let him really think about what he has done. Then if there is a second offense, have one hand surgically removed. If there is a third offense, have the remaining hand surgically removed. I think after the second offense, you won't see him again. Oh, I almost forgot—you rights activists, stay the hell out of it.

Now I would like to give my opinion on the homeless population. I do believe there could be a couple ways one might end up homeless, but I also know there are a lot of ways to get help. In our town, I see homeless people who are boozers and drug heads. They hang out downtown in our parks and scare the hell out of people. Our county provides a free clean needle exchange for people shooting up. It's nice to take a walk downtown in the parks only to see used needles on the ground or a drug addict being revived by a police officer or paramedics. The free needle exchange program is working for the drug addicts but not the taxpayers. The police are called to the parks all the time for fights, drugs, and vandalism, and yet activists want to call them homeless and feel sorry for these people. What we need to do is throw their asses in jail with bread and water, give them a chance to detox, let them out, and tell them to get jobs. If there is a problem again, take them to jail again—but take away the bread and water. We need to clean this up. There are too many opportunities for these people to survive in this country. We don't need this, and we wouldn't have it if we would just do something about it. You have to realize these types of people know that our laws are soft and that they can get by with what they do. It's time to stop it. You have to want to help yourself, and the majority of these people don't want to help themselves. So what do you do? The only thing I can come up with is tougher laws. When you provide too much help for these types of people, they take advantage of it. Now again, remember this is only my opinion about what I see and hear going on across this country. It's been a long time since we have seen an economy do what this one is starting to do, so maybe this will help this problem.

One other problem we need to stop and make illegal is these people standing at street corners with signs looking for free handouts. To start with, I don't know how they get the courage to do this, but from what I understand, they make pretty good money. It makes our towns look bad. In my town where they stand, there are signs posted all around them for help wanted. This tells me they are too lazy to work. One thing I think I may see with this problem that is a lot of the jobs today state you must have a high school diploma or GED. Well, if it is hard to get help, would you take what you can get? There are a lot of people out there who don't have a diploma or GED and are probably even better workers than some people who do have them. I also believe everyone needs an education. Again, this is only my opinion, and I'm trying to think of things that might help.

The best quote I think I have ever heard was, "Ask not what your country can do for you—ask what you can do for your county." I believe JFK would have possibly been the best president this county could have had, had he not been shot.

Now, I would like to talk a little about the many children being born and having to be raised by only one parent; in most cases, this is the mother. You young kids today, this is a terrible decision you make, and it hurts the children the most. Why would you ever have a child before you have your own life intact? This is one of the problems with the welfare system. This is a bad decision you young parents both make, and it ends up costing the taxpayers. I think there should be some type of law that says you must be able to support a child in order to have a child. Why should taxpayers pay you to support your child? I know this all comes down to both parents making terrible decisions that hurt the children the most. It's terrible to see children have to grow up this way because it affects these children not only today but for their entire lives. The way of life has changed so much from when I was a kid. You never heard about this fifty years ago, but now it happens everywhere and all the time. I think if these kids are underage and make a decision like this, then you have to choose to hold their parents financially accountable rather than making it the taxpayers' burden. We need to do something to stop young people from making these mistakes.

GUN CONTROL

Let's talk a little about gun control. I think we can all agree that you are never going to get all the guns off the street. What I think we need to agree on is that guns don't kill. It is the people who use these guns who kill. Owing guns have a lot of different meanings to people. There is the gun collector, the person who likes to hunt, the person who likes to target practice, and many other reasons why a people own guns. It is the criminals who make this a problem. I believe a lot of people own guns for protection from criminals. Maybe some of you reading this book remember when you could just leave your doors unlocked or keys in your car and not worry about someone stealing your stuff. It's a shame that we live in a world where you have to worry so much about theft. I believe what has caused this problem are the drugs and the drug dealers bringing drugs here. We never protected our borders, and we now have a president who wants to build the wall to protect this county—yet some crazy-ass people want to fight him over this. Can you not see that most of the problems with theft and violence that are going on in this country are because of drugs, and that most drugs come from Mexico? Why the hell is this not clear to the people who want to fight Mr. Trump over this?

If we build the wall and protect the borders, we stop that part of the drugs coming in. Then all we have to do is deal with the drug dealers and addicts who are here making this crap, and a lot of the crime will stop. Don't you see this? It is common sense. Wouldn't it be great to start hearing that crime is coming down in this country?

Most crime happens because of drugs. Most gun crimes happen because of drugs, and people either kill for money to buy more drugs, or they get killed because they didn't pay for the drugs. Doesn't it make sense to do what we have to do to stop the drugs? Most crimes happen because of drugs, and most gun crimes happen because of drugs. Doesn't it make sense to do what we have to do to stop the damned drugs? From all of my research, all other countries protect their borders. Let this president protect our border. Instead, we offer free needle exchanges and then find them all over the streets, and we spend all this money to use Narcon to bring these drug addicts back to life just so they can do it again. Who the hell thinks of all this? Why don't we put this money toward building the wall and stopping the drugs from coming in? Now again, remember that this is only my opinion. I'm sure some of these people need help, but as I see it, you have two choices in life: choose to do the right thing, or choose to do the wrong thing. I don't understand why anyone would choose to do drugs. There absolutely cannot be any way that is good choice. You have never heard of any good coming out of anything or anyone who has chosen to have drugs in his life. Maybe the bad people sell it because of the money, but at the same time, they have to be living in fear of being caught. What kind of life can this be? If you are a drug addict reading this book, let the drugs go. There are many other great choices you can make in life.

Let me say one thing that really got me on the drug problem: I love country music and listen to a lot of artists, and the one artist that I always thought had the most beautiful voice and the greatest female singe of all time was Whitney Houston. Every time I think of her life ending because of drugs, I find it sad and unbelievable. I think about how this woman brought a lot of joy into many homes with her voice, and to think she is gone at such a young age because of drugs is very sad. This is just one terrible instance. Imagine how many people have lost their lives because of drugs. I'm telling you if we get this wall built on the border, we will stop a lot of the drugs from coming into the country.

Now, let me give my two cents worth on the disease called cancer. Back when I was a kid, one didn't hear much about this disease, and now it takes so many lives. I bet there is not one person out there who can't say someone in his or her family has died of cancer. Now, remember, this is only my opinion. The first thing I would like to say is I can't believe we haven't found a cure for this yet. What I think has happened is it's related to all this crap they spray on crops to make them grow bigger or greener or faster, or to kill insects and crop-related diseases. All I know is we didn't do this years ago, and we didn't hear about cancer. We hear a lot about how this is not good for you, and I don't think they really know. One minute something is good for you, and the next minutes it's bad for you. All these additives are put in our food products to make them last longer, look better, taste better, or have more color. I think if you want to be healthy, you need to have your own garden and grow your own vegetable to eat and to can. I eat a lot of hamburger. I am finding that when I buy hamburger and don't cook it within a day, then it spoils. Maybe we need our own cows with our own gardens. It seems more people are taking up canning or buying organic.

Another topic I want to talk about is animal cruelty. It is very sad to drive down the road and see a dog chained to a tree or post with no shelter or food or water in sight. Or when I see a horse standing in the rain in a field that is nothing but mud because it doesn't have any shelter, I ask myself what kind of person would do this to an animal. I've never been able to come up with an answer because this is a horrible thing to do to an animal. These animals are helpless, and one wants to stop and cut the chain or let the horse out to be free. Then there are reports of people who own twenty or more cats or dogs, and the animals are found in terrible living conditions. I ask myself what makes people do this to these animals. In my opinion, a person who abuses an animal must have mental problems. There should be laws against animal abuse, and if a person is convicted, the punishment should fit the crime. If you take a moment and do an Internet search on animal cruelty, you will see all the cases and how much of it is going on. If you ever find yourself with a little extra time or money, volunteer your time to your local animal shelter or make a financial donation.

HEALTH CARE

Now, remember: this is only my opinion, but I have thoughts on our healthcare and why it's such a mess. This seems to be one of the things, and everyone is not sure what to do about it. One thing that I see wrong with it is the cost that the doctors and hospitals are allowed to charge. After some research and stories, I've been told the cost for an ambulance ride can be around two thousand dollars. How is this possible? Oh, and if you think that's crazy, did you know one Tylenol can cost you twenty-five dollars while in the hospital? Also, the average cost for one night's stay in the hospital is over four thousand dollars. These are just a few things that I see wrong with the health care system. The cost of these items is crazy, and that is why health care for everyone is so expensive. It seems like people with insurance help cover the costs for the people who don't have insurance. I would like to think that the first thing they should do is lower these prices. Come up with a fair price for these health care items and then let the insurance companies bid on them; that way, your best price goes to the customer. The way it looks now, all who are involved can charge whatever they want. Well, anyway, that's the best I have on this subject. Let's hope it all works out for everyone.

SPORTS

I would like to talk a little about sports. First, what's up with this kneeling when we are honoring our country? I'm pretty sure this all started with one guy. Is there not a better way for you get some attention? Other than dishonoring our flag, you could have tried doing something great on the field—something you are getting paid to do. I believe your bad judgment has made you unemployed.

Now, back to the sport of football. They seem to be changing the way football has been played since its beginning by adding too many rules and regulations. As some of the players themselves have said recently, football is a sport where you are going to get hit, and it's probably going to hurt. If you don't want to get hit or hurt, then don't play football. Doesn't this seem simple? These players are paid unbelievable amounts of money due to this, and they should know what the risks are going in. I do agree with the concussion rule, but it should be up to the players how far they wants to torture their bodies.

What seems crazy to me is boxing and the UFC. These guys get in there and beat each other's brains out, but nobody says anything about it. Don't take away what football is. It's always been a contact sport. Don't turn it into a sissy's game. We fans love the sport and don't want to see anyone get hurt, but the players know it is a contact sport. Like I said before, if you don't want to get hit, then find another sport to play.

Let me say this one more time about the kneeling issue. Please find another way to get attention to whatever your issue is other than dishonoring our flag, our country, and our veterans. This was horrible to watch, and to think it was started by one person who used the wrong thing to get attention. We all know who he is and what happened to him for doing it. Some of the other sports teams tried doing it, but I think they finally said this isn't right. I believe this nonsense has finally stopped, and for that we thank you. I want to commend NASCAR for keeping it out of what is often called the American sport, stock car racing, but I've never seen or heard anyone wanting to do it in that sport anyway.

Speaking of NASCAR, let's talk about how much this sport has changed. Think about this for a little bit. A few years ago, the stands at almost all tracks were full. At Bristol Motor Speedway, they always had a waiting list one had to get on just to buy tickets. Now, remember what I say is only my opinion, but I'm talking about this because this because how much has changed. The really good drivers were in the early years, when they drove these cars fast as they did with very little safety equipment. Back then it was a Ford, Chevy, or Dodge, or whatever make of car, and they had to make that car perform especially well due to their driving skills. These cars today practically drive themselves, and there is minor risk of getting hurt in them anymore. I remember watching interviews with Dale Earnhardt, and he was asked about his open-face helmet and safety issues. His reply was something along the lines that that this stuff was for sissies as a driver, you know the risks, and if you don't want to take a chance that you could get killed, then a person shouldn't race. I believe had he not gotten killed, he would have quit before he wore all the safety devices drivers wear today. I see so many empty seats now, and I'm not sure how NASCAR is going to get the fans back. After this year, most all of the big-name drivers are gone, and they have these cars that are all the same; I can't tell a Ford from a Chevy when they are out there on the track.

My opinion is that too many rules and regulations have killed the sport. I understand some of them, and you should have some regulations, but there are too many in this sport. They have taken it away from the crew chief or mechanic. I used to spend anywhere from three to five hours every Sunday watching NASCAR racing. Now I will watch a race every once in a while. When I began watching NASCAR, I followed Jeff Gordon. I'm a big fan of his. I first saw Jeff racing a sprint car on a quarter-mile track here in Bloomington, Indiana. I believe he was only fifteen years old at the time. From that point on, I said to myself, "That kid is going to be a hell of a race car driver. When he got into NASCAR, he and Ray were unbelievable. Had they not changed the point system the way they did, Jeff would have had the most championships ever. When I started following Jeff's career, I was also buying all the merchandise that came out, which means I was buying die-casts of all kinds, T-shirts, jackets, and more. I was buying it and thinking that someday this stuff would be worth a lot of money. Now I can hardly give it away. I'm not sure what went wrong with this, but I can tell you I have a lot of it. I hope they can turn this sport around and make it as exciting as it used to be.

I now watch the Indy Racing League (IRL). Although a lot of your big-name drivers have left this sport too, the action is still good. These cars are very fast, and the drivers put on a good show. My favorite driver is Helio Casternevez. Not only is he a good driver, but he is funny, interviews well, and always smiles. It seems to me that these race car team owners are looking for young drivers now, and this is in the IRL and NASCAR. It is sad to see the big-name drivers disappear. I also think that the main reason for this is the money: they don't have to pay these younger drivers as much as they would the big-name drivers.

I guess I'm just getting old, and it is hard to watch the changes that are going on. I wrote this book because of all the changes that are going on in this country.

Again, I never thought I would ever be sitting here writing a book, but I'll tell you it gives you a lot of time to think. I think once you hit fifty, you begin to think differently. I know I have, and I look at how much time I have left, what I've done with these fifty years I've been here, and I should do with the time I have left. As you know, none of us have any idea how much time we have on earth, and I think the age of fifty made me start thinking about it. I do know one thing, and that is I don't believe we've ever had a better chance in this county to do great things and become great again with the president we have now, Mr. Trump. Mr. Trump is going to do great things.

I would like to speak about the Mexicans for just a little bit. In my business, I see a lot of Mexican workers. They do a lot of the roofing work, drywall work, and painting in my town. I don't have a problem with this as long as they are here legally. One of the big problems I have with this is they don't speak our language. I think one of the rules to become legal here should be you must speak English. I took the time last week to drive through our town because there is a lot of construction work going on right now. I stopped by a few building sites just to look, and what I saw at every sight was unbelievable. Approximately 80 percent of all workers were Mexicans. I sat in my truck and thought, *Where are all the American workers?* In my business, I have had three conversations with other builders, and we have seen that there aren't any new, younger builders coming up in this field that is in our area. There are not many builders left who have been in this area for most of my life. I wonder who is going to build homes for the future generations. I also wonder why there are not any new, younger builders coming into this trade. Now, I don't know if it's like this all over this country, but I do see it here.

Back to the Mexicans again. I don't see a problem with this as long as they have come here legally and are paying taxes like they are supposed to do. I know with the union jobs downtown that these companies are using Mexican workers due to cheaper wages. I do believe this is illegal, but who checks on this, and what is done when they find this to be the truth? Is this why there are so many fewer Americans in the trade? Have they been forced out due to paying Mexicans less money? If so, this is very wrong, and our government needs to be watching this very closely. It takes schooling and skill to build these buildings and homes properly, and I personally see a lot of bad construction these days. If you can't even talk to these people in English to explain to them the right way, then what do you think you're going to get? The bottom line is we let this happen by not protecting our borders. You have to see that letting these illegal people in here has hurt this country and put it in a bad way. We have to send these people back and put them in line to come back here legally. They knew they were coming here illegally, and now it is time to do it right.

We have to stand up for our laws just like other counties do, especially Mexico. This makes me so mad when I see these idiots on TV making statements like "You can't do that to these people." I say it is time to put America first, like Mr. Trump is trying to do. You all should come to your senses, leave our president alone, and let him do this for all of us. Just like he says, we should make America great again. I believe no matter what you Democrats try to do, Mr. Trump is going to get the job done. We need this for our country, and Mr. Trump knows this.

HOLLYWOOD

If I may, I would like to speak a little about Hollywood. First of all, I don't know how you celebrities all become Democrats, but when you are performing either acting or singing, do you think that the audience, either at home watching you on TV or live at your big concert, are all Democrats? How many times have you actually thought about this? Let me tell you from my own experiences just since Mr. Trump was elected. There are several of you whom I either watch in movies or listen to via CD because of your talent and not because of whether you are a Democrat or Republican. Now after I've seen how you have treated Mr. Trump, I look at you and say, "I can't believe this person is really this way." You people have made the American dream through Democrats and Republicans buying tickets that made you people very rich, and I can't belie you carry on the way you do.

It is absolutely amazing what Mr. Trump has been able to do to become the president of the United States. Why put him down? It doesn't make any sense to me. Again, why would we not simply support him through his term and see what he can do for us? Do you think you would have made it where you are today without the support you have gotten? Hell, no. Again, it took Democrats and Republicans to fill these seats and make you people famous. This is why I keep saying, "Why can't we just get along?" It doesn't make any damned sense to me. Can't you imagine how great it would be if both parties would just get along?

Remember one very important point of mine. I never watched your movie or listened to your CD because you were a Democrat or

10

Republican; I was a fan because of your talent. It also seems to me that the most drama going on out there is your very own Democratic women molesters. I'm just saying what I see, and again, this is only my opinion; remember that I'm just an ordinary citizen. The 2019 Golden Globes Awards were on last night, and they just had Oprah give this big speech for the women who have been mistreated by men. I think this is a great thing she did, but come on. How did your fake media turn this into her running for president? Are you kidding me? Oh, and I see where one million fewer people watched the Golden Globes than last year. Does that tell you something? Remember what I said earlier: it wasn't just Democrat who made you all so rich.

It is very sad to me that we have to be so divided when we are all Americans. We should all come together, work together, and laugh together to make America great again. I see all these good things staring to finally happen for this country, and I wish we could all come together and enjoy this time in life together, knowing this is all going to be so much better for the next generation. Hey, I watch the news every day, and I'm hoping for the day that I can hear in the news the two parties are starting to get along, compromising on both sides, and making this country great again together. I wonder who on either side would not want this. I also ask myself, "Why would this fake media be so hard and nasty to people? Do they do this for the Democrats, or do they do this because they have nothing better to do? Who or what gets them to try to start so much bullshit?" Wouldn't it be better to report on things like the two sides sitting down yesterday and agreeing on something, or the fact that Mr. Trump is bringing jobs back to America? Don't these types of things sound better than all the crap they come up with? Sometimes I laugh at the crap they try to start because it's so unbelievable. Oh, and by the way, why are we not having anything on Matt Lauer, your lead media man who was so great and put down so many Republicans during his last twenty years? He tried to make Mr. Trump look so bad, and it turns out one of your best people is one of the worst. I can just imagine how much you all might be going on about this had Matt Lauer been a Republican; it would be all we would hear about.

I used to watch Matt Lauer and say to myself, "How can this guy be like he is to Republicans?" I guess you Democrats must have made him feel so good that you made him the way he is. But you sure didn't have much to say when the truth came out about one of your own, and now you have nothing. You all are shocked and can't believe how your own turned out to be the worst. Let me tell you this: I think this guy is a joke. I believe he too had the American dream and its money, and he thought he was above all. I thank the woman who came forward, brought down this horrible woman molester, and got his ass off TV.

I wonder whether these victims are Republicans? Just curious. I believe you people won't stay down for long. You all are going to realize how good Mr. Trump is for our country, and you are going to have to say we need to support him. Remember, he is doing this for everyone, not just the Republicans. You Democrats only back your own, and that is wrong. We are America, and damn it, we should get along.

WELFARE

L et's talk a little bit about welfare. We know one thing: there are a lot of people on welfare. I will say there are a few who probably need to be on welfare. I believe President Trump has already helped this number. The first thing I believe you have to do if you want welfare is be drug tested every thirty days; if you test positive for drugs in your system, then no more welfare. I truly believe if we had this as a rule, it would cut welfare in half. People who are on welfare receive their checks, and then they run to buy drugs, or they go to the casino. They should be ashamed of themselves.

This free service that America offers is one reason America is great, and I believe it is a reason some outsiders want to be here. A lot of this would stop if we would come up with a law stating you must prove you can afford a child in order to have a child. We have to do something to stop all these people who take advantage of welfare.

BRICK-AND-MORTAR STORES

We are now seeing a lot of the big-name stores closing. These are the stores we've known and shopped at for years: K-Mart, Sears, HH Gregg. I wonder what is happening in this new and changing world, and what is causing this. I just heard on the news that Wal-Mart is closing sixty stores of its Sam's Club stores. I wonder whether this is because of Internet sales helping or hurting the economy. It's getting hard to keep up with all these changes. The other day when I was in Wal-Mart, I saw that the store was full of shoppers, and I think I counted twenty-seven registers to check out. Only three registers were open, and then they had all these self-checkout lines. These self-checkout registers seem to be eliminating jobs, and if this is the case, is this good or bad? Or have they come up with this system because help is hard to find? Again, I want you to understand I'm not against these Mexican workers, and I do believe we need them. What I'm against is those who come here illegally. We have to uphold our laws, and Mr. Trump is trying his best to do this. We have to support him.

STATISTICS

I would now like to go over some very interesting statistics that I've wondered about. I decided I would look them up for you. These numbers are unbelievable, and I think you will agree. These subjects are a lot of what I have tried to hit. Let's start with cancer. As I said before, most of us know someone who has died of this or has had it, and the number is staggering. Over seven million die each year of cancer, and women make up the majority. When you hear a number like this, you think that is crazy. Why can't we find a cure for this disease? With all the technology we have, this makes no sense to me. Again, it's only my opinion, but I think it's all these chemicals we use to spray on crops and the food that comes across the borders. We need to stop this and hope there is a cure soon.

My next statistic is we have nearly four million babies born in the United States each year. They say about eleven thousand of them will die. With this number, I just hope they have both parents to raise them, and I hope the country is in good shape for their generation. Thank God we have a president right now who is trying to make this a better country.

One more horrible statistic is heart attacks. They say five hundred thousand people die each year of a heart attack. This is something I think will always be there because there are a lot of things that can cause this to happen. I lost both of my parents due to heart attacks.

Now, here is another statistic you probably don't know: murder. They say we have sixteen thousand murders each year in the United

States, and they also say about eleven thousand of these murders are caused by firearms. We know this is a terrible thing, and I'm sure drugs have a lot to do with this number, but remember that guns don't kill— people kill. Let's hope that when Mr. Trump gets the wall built and stops the drugs from coming here, this number will decline.

Here is another drug statistic for you. The number of drug deaths each year in the United States is about two hundred thousand. This is another number that I find unbelievable. Can you imagine two hundred thousand people dying every year due to drug-related deaths? I don't know which drugs or anything like that, and I'm sure you can do your own research, but just hearing a number like this is staggering. Again, we now have a president who is trying to do something about our drug problem, and the crazy Democrats want to stop him.

SMOKING

Here's another statistic that might make you think. The number of smoking deaths is crazy. They say around four hundred thousand people die each year from smoking. As a former smoker myself, this number is unbelievable. Smoking is a very bad addiction. I know, because one of the hardest things I've ever done was quit smoking. As for my opinion on this problem, I believe there is tough education out there for someone to see that this is bad for you, and you simply have to have the willpower to quit.

ALCOHOL

Now on another statistic, and that is alcohol. The number of deaths each year for this is one hundred thousand people. This is another subject where there is plenty of education out there, and you just have to be able to control your drinking and use the right judgment. The worst thing about alcohol is when you drink and then drive. The statistic for deaths in the United States caused by a drunk driver is a little over ten thousand people. When you make this terrible decision to do this and kill someone, then you have to do the time. To me, this is probably one of the dumbest decisions you can ever make considering all your other options. I can't even imagine spending the rest of my life behind bars for drinking. Call a cab or a friend. Don't allow this to happen to you. Of all fatal vehicle crashes, 28 percent were alcohol related. The good thing is these numbers have been coming down year by year, so let's think right and keep this number down.

THEFT

Here is a subject that gets to me the most: theft. The statistic is over twelve million thefts per year in the United States. These people who steal your belongings are no good. I'm telling you they are the worst, and those who have had something stolen will tell you how mad it makes them. Again, my opinion is our laws are terrible for this crime, and it's why you hear "Once a thief, always a thief." People can get charged with theft, and then it is too easy for them to get out of jail. Most thieves are repeat offenders.

We need to do something about this, and there has to be a law with harsh enough consequences that a person will think twice before taking something that doesn't belong to him or her. For those people who don't agree to this, I'm thinking you'll change your mind when theft happens to you. It is getting so bad that thieves are stealing anything and anywhere they can. Remember that these people are no good and too lazy to get a real job, earn their places in the world, and be productive citizens. We have to change our laws, and we have a president who will do this and get it done.

MARRIAGE AND DIVORCE

There are around two million marriages each year, but eight hundred thousand divorces are granted every year in the United States. This is a sad statistic. That is a staggering number for divorces, and it makes me wonder what the problem is. Why is this number so high? Is the time coming where you won't hear any more about couples celebrating their sixty-year wedding anniversary? Are couples marrying too fast? What happened to "till death do us part"? I do know times are changing and the world is different. I don't believe marriage or families will ever be the same. I think the times have changed too much. I guess all I can say is to make sure he or she is the right person before you tie the knot.

As I'm writing this book, I am switching back and forth between CNN and Fox News. The government has just shut down. I also just read that Mexico had a record number of murders this past year, and the number is unbelievable: over twenty-nine thousand. We just shut down our government because the Democrats want to keep all these illegal people here. What the hell is wrong with these people? You Democrats just shut down our government and put our troops and some of our government employees in a position where they are not sure they will get paid. You Democrats just put illegals ahead of our own citizens. Our president knows that we have to have this wall and stop all this crap from coming into our country, but you keep fighting him over this. I can't believe it. If the job of our president is to protect us, and that's what he is trying to do, why do some of you people want to stop him from doing this?

I think I've figured out some of the problem. We need to put terms on our elected officials—the same terms as what is on our president. I think some of you people need to go (Pelosi) and get some new people in there who have the same intention as Trump: to make America great again. I'm going to ask you nonbelievers to watch Hannity on Fox News one time, and you will hear the truth about all the dirtiness the Democrats are doing. We need to put America and Americans first.

I may just be an ordinary citizen, but I tell you I see all of this as it is. I truly believe we can all come together, back our president, and make this country great again. There has to be a part of you Democrats who sit there and think, "Maybe President Trump really means what he says. Maybe he can do this. Maybe we should back him."

And one more thing. I'm just a citizen of this country, and I can see what caused most of our problems is the border with the illegals crossing and coming over here, as well as all the drugs that come into our country and cause so much devastation to this country and to our citizens. Please let the president build the wall and start making this country what it can be. Let him drill for oil, build pipelines, and stop depending on anyone else to supply oil to this country. Mr. Trump can do this, and we all can come together and, with Mr. Trump's leadership, make this one hell of a great country. Now, remember this book is my opinion on what I see as today's problems in the country. I want to support what I think to be the greatest president this country has ever seen.

I just watched Mr. Trump speak out in Pennsylvania. He spoke about how great things are now up to this point, and he now has been president for fourteen months. You have to believe that what he is doing for this country is incredible. The big news right now is that Mr. Trump is going to meet with North Korea and their terrible leader. That has never happened like this before, and it can possibly be the greatest thing that has ever happened for this country and all others. But once again, this unbelievable media is not giving any credit at all to Mr. Trump for another great thing that he is making happen. All they want to say is, "Well, any president could have done this." I say, "Then why the hell haven't they done this?" I'm telling you people again: if you want the truth and really want to know what is going on in this country, then you have to watch Fox News.

Mr. Trump talked about a lot of things tonight, and I want to speak about a few of them. One is sanctuary cities that want to protect the criminals. Why the hell would any of you elect someone that wants this for your city? Do you not understand how wrong this is and how dangerous this is for your own family and friends? Who the hell are these elected people who think they can go against our own government and our laws? I can tell you that with Mr. Trump as president, I don't think they will get away with it for very long. I can also say that when these cities stop getting any government funding, they will change their minds. Let's see who wins this fight. You know, this shouldn't be a problem anyway. You have to stop electing these kinds of people who are going to do things to hurt this country. Again, I just don't know why we have to have this kind of crap going on. Why can't we just get along and do the things that are right for the country?

In just fourteen months, we can see that Mr. Trump has done and is doing what he said he would do during the debates. This is one of the big reasons he was elected. Can you believe it? We finally have someone in there who is actually doing what he said he would do— and more. Another point he hit on tonight is that there are now more people employed than ever in the history of this county. With that fact alone, we should all be in great support of this man. It is a damned shame that this fake news media will not get their act together, back this president, and tell it the way it is. I'm thinking right now, "What in the hell are they going to come up with tomorrow? What kind of people really believe this crap that they come up with?" I see what is on CNN and other stations like it—who the hell listens to this stuff? I'm one who understands you have to have two parties to get things done and keep things fair for everyone, but it's a damned shame when the Democrats are for themselves alone. I truly believe at some point, because Mr. Trump is doing so well, the Democrats are going to have to come aboard because what will they have left?

Another of the other great points Mr. Trump hit on tonight are drug dealers. If you were listening, Mr. Trump asked other countries whether they had drug problems, and their reply was they had zero tolerance for drugs; if a drug dealer was caught, then the drug dealer got the death penalty. I spoke about this earlier and did my own research, and I told you what their laws were. As you see, these other countries don't seem to have drug or theft problems. I would love to be the leader of this, but let's get behind Mr. Trump and make our own laws on drugs and theft, with zero tolerance. Then we can all sleep better at night. Can you imagine how great it would be to know that our country also has no problem? Take a moment and think about it.

It is so great to finally see this country going in the right direction, and I can't wait to see what this country is going to be like by 2024, when Mr. Trump is done with making American great again. Let me say again that I've never written anything before in my life, and I apologize if this book jumps around a little bit. To give you an idea, I'm in my seventh month of writing this right now, and I have to do this at night because I'm very busy running my business, but I am enjoying this. I watch Hannity at 9:00 p.m. every night to get the truth about everything so that I can write this with the best knowledge I can get. I'm amazed at how much is going on right now and how much Mr. Trump is getting accomplished, and it is giving me a lot of pleasure to write about it. You know what would be fun? In about four years from now, I hope I'm able to write another book and call it *I Can't Believe How Great We Are Getting Along.*

Now, it's just a damned shame that I have to talk about this, but let's discuss this school shooting in Florida. First of all, we have to stop these kids from doing their walkouts. This is only happening because of the Democrats trying to get their votes. This was a terrible tragedy and should have never happened, but again, it wasn't the gun; it was a mental person who would have gotten hold of a gun no matter what. Here is the biggest problem with this situation: it could have been prevented had the FBI or the local police done their job. It's been revealed that they had been called with complaints on this person almost forty times and done nothing to stop this mental person from hurting anyone. The students should be marching to have these officials who did nothing be fired. We need to teach that guns are not the problem; it is the crazy people out here. When you see or know something, you have to say something—and when it is reported, the officials must follow up on the report. What a shame that something like this happened when it could have been easily prevented. It is also a shame that Democrats take advantage of a situation like this just to try to get votes. If you watched Shawn Hannity on Fox News, he said it best. We need to have retired police officers or veterans at all of our schools, armed to protect these students. Let these people pay no taxes. You have to see that this makes perfect sense, and we would never have this problem again. Let's also do this right now and not let it sit in some office for years for debate. Get it done now.

As you may know, I work a little on this book and then may not write again for two or three weeks. However, I watch Fox News every night at 9:00 p.m., which is Hannity's show, and I honestly think I could write for a year nonstop with everything I hear there. I am not sure how you Democrats think the way you do. Mr. Trump has this country doing so well right now, and you can't say a good word about it at all. You and this fake news can only look for bad things and make things up. I can't believe what I hear out of you all.

Now, I'm very concerned with what has just happened with the budget bill that Mr. Trump has just signed. I hate to slap it, but our own Republicans did not help our president very much on this deal. I honestly didn't think Mr. Trump would have signed this budget bill, but I'm guessing he didn't have a choice. As we all know, Mr. Trump campaigned on the border wall, and there was no money in this bill for the new border wall, which we all know we need to have in order to stop drugs and these illegals from coming into our country. It is unbelievable that you people would put the president in this situation.

I truly believe that Mr. Trump has a plan to still get this wall built. I know as hard as he campaigned on this and as bad as he wants it, he has to have some kind of plan. I have no idea what might be his plan, but I don't believe he will let this go or let you crazy people stop him. Why in the hell are we giving this president so much trouble for trying to protect this country and keep Americans safe?

We've had our own border people tell us that we need this wall to stop all the drugs and illegals from coming in here, so why are we not getting this done? Why would any of you not want this to happen? I can only hope that this comes back to bite you people in the ass. I'm going to stand behind this president and hope that he can make it past all the bullshit he has to deal with from Democrats. I watch Fox News and listen to all this political crap that goes on every day, and I have to wonder just what is going to happen and where this country is going to end up. We finally have a president who is trying like hell to make this a great country again and stop other countries from screwing us. I have to wonder who is going to come in after Mr. Trump. It is a very scary thing to think about. I can say this to Mr. Trump: keep firing the ones who don't agree with you and won't back your agenda. You will eventually get all the right people on your side to help you make this a great country again.

I haven't written for a few days again due to being very busy with my business. This economy is great right now, and there is a lot of work out there. I'm getting so damned mad at these Democrats. I'm going to have to get this book finished because I can't stand what these Democrats are doing. Let me talk about this a little bit. Number one, they are clearly using these illegal people in our country for votes. How in the hell can you be so wrong about something that is so obvious? These people came here illegally, and they need to go get in line and do it right. The bottom line is that you Democrats have to be stopped because this has gone too far. At some point, there has to be enough of you to see this clearly and get behind what is right for this country.

One thing that would stop a lot of this crap is that we need to put term limits on politicians and get their asses out of office. I believe it is no different than term limits for the president. You unbelievable people are using these kids and hope to get their future vote instead of teaching them that it's not guns that kill but crazy people. You damn Democrats have tried everything to hurt Mr. Trump, and nothing has worked to this point. Now you use what I call the pro-state to try to hurt him for something that, coming from Stormy Daniels, was consensual twelve years ago. This has nothing to do with running this country, but you people will not stop. Anderson Cooper, you looked like a damned idiot while you were interviewing her. It's a damned shame that with all that is going on in the world, this is whom you choose to interview. Unbelievable. Where was the media when President Clinton did all this lying and cheating? And then there was the Cigar Act. Where the hell was the fake as news then?

You people should be talking about all the good Mr. Trump is doing for this country and how well the economy is doing. I personally can't remember the economy doing this good ever. Here in my hometown, we have a medical company called Cook Pharmica, and they are our largest employer. They are getting ready to expand and broke ground on the new site. The CEO of Cook said he is worried about being able to find enough employees. One of my points about this is that we can use these foreigners, and we have the work for them. They simply need to come here legally to live the American dream. Mr. Trump said it best: he knows we need them, but he wants to get rid of the bad ones. The damned media should report on things that are good for this country, not all of the bullshit. There is absolutely no sense in this. It's gone too far, and I'm personally sick of hearing all the crap you people keep coming up with. I keep hoping and wishing at some point we could all get along, but now I'm not sure it will ever happen. You people stoop so low that all republicans can do is keep on with the agenda of keeping America and our citizens first. They will try to deal with these crazy Democrats the best they can. Hopefully enough of you Democrats will cross over and support this president and this country. I'll say this to Mr. Trump: I don't know how you are getting so much done and having to deal with so much fake news and bull crap from the Democrats, but thank you. We are behind you all the way.

Now we are having a problem with the census question that asks, "Are you an American citizen?" These damn Democrats want to fight this because they are afraid of losing votes. You should have to show your American citizenship ID to be able to vote or do anything in this country. I wish you people could see how stupid you look and sound on TV. Thank God for people like Shawn Hannity, who keeps the truth out there every night. If a lot of you people would watch and listen to him, you would know exactly what the truth is. I just finished watching *The Laura Ingraham Show*, which comes on right after Hannity on Fox News, and she showed a lot of recent crimes around the country that these illegal people are committing. It is terrible. And to think that you damn Democrats are backing these kinds of people just because you need votes. Laura Ingraham is another show you need to watch in order to hear the truth of what is going on in this country.

Another thing that is very hard to believe is the sanctuary cities thinking they don't have to follow the federal laws of this country. How does this happen, and how does this continue? This is only my opinion, and I have never written anything before, but I tell you this is unbelievable and very hard to watch. I believe now it is time to stop writing and hope that everything will be able to stay on track for Mr. Trump. I truly believe he is the best chance this country has ever had, and I can only hope that a lot of you nonbelievers can come around and start believing that this is the best chance America has ever had. We are being led by the best president this country has ever had. Again, let's give him a chance, and just maybe this will be the greatest country ever. To all of you who take the time to read this, I thank you and wish you all the best.

I just watched the first State of the Union address from Mr. Trump, and I've got to tell you that I cannot believe the way the Democrats acted. I believe this is the worst I've ever seen from one party in the time I've been alive. The economy is really coming back, these companies are coming back, and the new tax bill is doing great things for businesses and individuals. I think one of the big items that Mr. Trump hit on is that the unemployment rate for black people is at its lowest in a long time—and yet these Democrats never stood or applauded. This is a president who is for all Americans, and everyone should be able to see this by now. What is wrong with these people who don't want to show any respect at all for what is happening? I've said it before and I'll say it again: imagine what Mr. Trump could do for this country if he didn't have to fight our own people, the Democrats. Can any of you imagine how great this country could be if we could all just get along? Every one of us has to start thinking America first. and what I mean is the illegals who are here. What I'm hearing from Mr. Trump is that they need to get in line, and if they are working here and paying taxes and have not committed any crimes, then they will be able to become residents of the

United States. If you are here and don't work or pay taxes, and you have caused trouble, then you need to leave and go back to where you came from. We all have to understand that this is out of control. Thank God that we finally have a president who is going to do something about this.

It's so simple: if you want to be here, then do it legally. I believe it is also very important that you learn our language, and this should be one of the requirements. This is the United States, and our language is English. The Democrats only care about the illegals because that is where they get most of their votes. We can all see that it's been a long time since we've seen America come alive and have someone stand up for us and fight for us. President Trump is letting these other countries know that we now are for America first. I see great things coming from what Mr. Trump is doing, and all I can hope for is that each and every day, he will gain more support.

One thing that concerns me most is the theft that is going on here in our own cities. I believe once we get rid of the illegals, this will help a lot, but I also believe that most of the theft is from drug heads needing more cash to buy drugs, and that is why they steal. These drug heads will have to get help when the new border wall is built, which will stop a lot of these drugs from coming here. Our laws have to be stronger on theft if we are going to stop it. These thieves are no good, and they have to be showed that if you steal, then you are going to pay dearly. Remember as you are reading this book that this is only my opinion, and I just want to get it out there. By the way, it would be great to hear from a few of you. Again, as I am writing this book, I have the local news on TV, and a story came on that was a very sad story, a death in Indianapolis. It is unbelievable that one of the Indianapolis Colts' players was killed by a supposedly drunk driver. The driver was reported as an illegal who had no driver's license and had already been deported two times. A young man had a great life ahead of him but is now dead, and a person is working a second job as an Uber driver, all because we didn't protect our borders. Yet you Democrats want to give these people a free ride? I think all you people need to speak to this young man's family and explain why you want to protect these types of people. Again, I know they all are not bad, however they need to come to the United States legally. This is just another reason Mr. Trump is trying to get this wall built and stop all of this from happening. You dumbasses need to stop fighting him. I don't like to talk this way, but when you hear those terrible stories and know how bad the illegals are, it makes me so mad knowing a small part of our country is fighting to keep them here.

Closing

These are just a few statistics I thought would be interesting to you. I feel they are also some of the problems in today's world. Remember again that my findings are through the Internet, and these are just my opinions and thoughts on the topics. I want you to hear from someone who is an ordinary citizen. I would like to close this book with why I think this president is a good choice, and how I wish we could all get along.

I'll say this again: I know in my lifetime, we have never had a better chance to receive and accomplish great things in America. Mr. Trump knows what this country needs to be great again. I know this because I watched and listened to the debates, and I listened to many interviews. He is a great businessman, not a politician. This president speaks his mind, and it drives the media and Democrats (and probably some Republicans) crazy. This man knows that it was wrong for our factories to go overseas. This man knows that our trades with other countries were wrong. This man knows that we must stop immigration. This man knows that we must build the wall to protect our borders. This man knows we have a one-sided, fake media. This man knows our health care is failing. This man knows our tax system is wrong. This man knows that the country was going downhill, and he knew he needed to run for president. This man knew there was not another person running who was going to do the right thing for America. This man knew that there are too many illegals here in this country, and something needs to be done about it. This man knows that we have to do something about the crime in our states. This man has taken care of all natural disasters that we have had since he took office. This man new that we are divided and need to come together to make American great again. This man knows our military was hurting, and he is building it back up. This man knows that our veterans were not being treated right, and he is changing this problem. This man knows that we must stop terrorists. This man will not take any crap from other countries. This man will fight to keep our jobs here. This man will drill and get oil from our own land. This man is going to defend our country like it has never been defended before.

The bottom line is we need to all come together as one, support this president, let him bring us back to a great country that we can be proud of. Other countries will look at us and follow suit. You nonbelievers need to watch Fox News and Shawn Hannity; it's there that you will get the facts and the truth.

We are now heading toward two years of Mr. Trump's presidency, and we just went through Memorial Day weekend. I went to the Indy 500. The place was packed, and I could see the difference in the economy. I went to the race because of two reasons. One, I'm a big Helio Castroneves fan, and it is supposed to be his last race there. I do not understand why Mr. Penske took his ride away from Helio. Helio is one of the greatest drivers who ever raced the Indy 500, and he loves that race; you can see it when he is being interviewed. I sure hope someone gives him a ride for next year's race. I believe he is one of the most liked guys in racing, and he has the greatest personality. I also went because through my business, we were given tickets to the race by one of the suppliers with whom we do business. With all that they did for us and hundreds of others, that tells you how good the economy is doing. What a great thing to see this all happening, and we all need to thank Mr. Trump for all that he is doing for this country.

This Memorial Day weekend is also my family reunion. How great it is to see my family. I spoke earlier about family and how much it has changed. This is my father's side of the family, and we are down to just two aunts left. Each year we see fewer family members show up. We need the next generation to step up and keep these reunions going. If we do not have family, then what do we really have? In today's world, we are wrapped up in so much that we forget about family and what it means to us. When I was growing up as a kid, everyone would go to Grandma's house on Sundays and special holidays for a big meal; it was simply the way it was, and I bet many of you can relate.

Try this at your next reunion. Have each person stand up, say his or her name and tell everyone what he or she is doing now. You will have a closer family relationship if you know what people are doing and where they're at. I truly believe families should stay close, but I have watched it get further and further away from what it should be. Again, we need the younger generation to step up and help keep families together.

I thought I would stop writing and try to end this book, but I have changed my mind. As you know, I'm writing only when I can find time. We are now heading for the November elections, and it is crazy what we are hearing coming from the news. At this point, which is now almost two years into Mr. Trump being in office, I have named the book *Why Can't We Just Get Along?* It probably should have been *How the Hell Can We Get Along?* I cannot believe what is going on. I believe the Democrats have lost their minds. How can losing power cause you to become so mean? You Democrats lost power because you are only for yourselves. The people saw this, decided it was time for a change, and got the hell away from you crazy people. I believe your actions are hurting you and your party and will have a long-term effect. You spend all your time trying to hurt or discredit Mr. Trump when you should be trying to come up with some kind of agenda for this country. Instead, you have nothing. You people think that the only way to get power back is to put down and hurt the ones now in power.

I will tell you it is not working, and I highly praise Mr. Trump for how he is still getting everything done while having to deal with crazy Democrats. I want to talk about this for a little bit because I have never thought we would ever see anything like it. Let me say this again: if you would put term limits on these politicians, then you would not have these problems. It is as if Chuck, Nancy, and Maxine believe they own the Democrats, but they are just hurting them. To make your party strong again, you need to get rid of these people. These three people have separated the parties so much and have made this world of politics so ugly. They have been in office too long, and it has gone to their heads. They are serving for all the wrong reasons. It's okay to disagree, but to hate each other is just wrong. We now have a great economy and many things that are going right for this country. Why can't not we get along? When now talking to these three people, they are very mean and won't settle for anything but having their power back. I think it is going to backfire on them.

We have a great president now who wants what is right for this country, and he cares for the people of this country. Donald Trump fights for this country, and he knows what it takes to make America great again. We just went through the midterms, and all the candidates whom Mr. Trump took the time to rally for won. We held the Senate, but the Democrats took the House.

I still do not understand why you would vote for Democrats who do not want the right things for you or this country. They only care about themselves and power. Winning the Senate was big, and it will still let the president get many things done that he wants to do. We will have to deal with Nancy Pelosi as House speaker again, but all I can think of is maybe you people who voted that way will get tired of listening to her and will see they have nothing to offer you and have no plans to improve America. After the past six months watching the news every night and reading the paper ever day about how these Democrats want to make our lives miserable, I no longer see things the way I did.

I think there are two reasons why you would be a Democrat. One is you have plenty of money and so don't care what happens. The other is you are poor because you are lazy, and you get all the free assistance that is offered. We are two years into this Mueller investigation at the taxpayers' expense, and it goes on and on. It's so hard to believe. For those who watch Fox News, the news that tells you the facts, you now know that the biggest crime ever committed in this country was done by Hillary Clinton and her gang by trying to keep Mr. Trump from being elected. They have all the facts on what Hillary did, but we are dealing with Mueller trying everything he can to find something on Mr. Trump. If the tables were turned, you would see unbelievable things happening. Now that we have a new attorney general coming in, I hope that he will have a special council come in, investigate all the crooked things that Hillary has done, and bring her and the Democrats involved to justice. The damned media that is only behind Democrats will not tell you the truth, and neither will they say a word about the illegal things that Hillary has done. If you would watch Hannity and Fox News, you would hear the facts and see how bad it really is.

I think that other countries must sit back and laugh at how we get along with each other and treat one another. You would think we could do a much better job at the way we treat each other. The United States is supposed to be the best place in the world, however we treat each other like hell. It makes no sense why we can't get along. We the people elect a new president every four to eight years no matter what. During that time, you would think no matter what, we all would back this president and help make a great country to be in. It's not just for us but our children too. We do have a great country, and we should make the most of it. We, as Democrats or Republicans, are elected on ideas regarding how we can improve this country, but we spend most of our time putting down each other. Can you tell me how this help us?

Many of our laws need to be changed. I believe the only way to stop all this hate is to put term limits on all elected officials. This would get people like Pelosi and Schumer out of there. We have a president who is trying very hard to make this country great again, and all they do is try to stop him. How does this help this country or the people in it? They look stupid when you see them on TV fighting this president. We just went through Christmas, and Mr. Trump had to shut down the government because they wouldn't give him the money for the border wall. What sense does this make? This wall is meant to keep America safe. Did any of us ever think about the job the border patrol people have? How would you like to get up every morning knowing you had to go stop illegals trying to enter this country, as well as stop illegal drugs from coming in here? This has to be a terrible and dangerous job. Do you think Pelosi and Schumer care about these people? Do you ever hear them say anything about our border people? Hell, no, they do not care—because they have walls around their homes. Mr. Trump cares about the people of this country and our border patrol officers, and he said he will fight for this wall. I believe him. It is a great thing knowing we have a president who is fighting for our safety. All you see out of these Democrats is fight, fight, fight against this wall and this president. My belief is that most of you people only see the fake news, which does not give you the truth. That is why we have so much disagreement in this country. If the media was honest the way they are supposed to be, we would not see so much disagreement.

One of my hopes in life before I go is that we as Americans Democrats and Republicans can someday get along and make America great together. That's the way it should be. Someone should start a new law to have term limits on politicians. I am telling you this would stop a lot of this crap that is going on. We have term limits on the president, and so should all elected officials.

Have you seen how bad the media and Democrats treat Melania Trump? This is a disgrace. You didn't see them do this to Michele Obama, did you? Melania has more intelligence than all of them put together, and they know it and cannot stand it. Oh, and she's a lot prettier. Hannity had Melania on his Christmas show special, and it was great to watch as she showed how much she appreciated our troops. She and Mr. Trump have went to their bases and ships and wherever they needed to go in order to let them know how much they mean to our country. That means a lot to these troops. Hannity showed a lot of this live, and she let our troops' families know how much we appreciate their sacrifice. God bless you, Melania. You are a treat as first lady.

We are going on about six days of the government shutdown because Schumer and Pelosi do not want this country or the people in it protected from the illegals and the drugs coming across our borders. The problem I see with this is that thousands of government employees are not being paid. Don't you think if the government shut down, these politicians should not be paid either? You see, this is the problem. If they were not paid, then there would not be a shutdown. These politicians would sit down together and make a deal. My point is you can see they care only about themselves.

To my other point, if we would set term limits on these politicians, we would not have these problems. Now, our taxes are paying these people to spend their time worrying about their power when they should be working for us on and making decisions for this country.

Can you only imagine the money that is being thrown away on the witch hunt trying to find something on Mr. Trump? What a waste of our time and money. If they only knew how stupid they look. You people who voted for these kinds of people can't possibly be happy with your decision. Would it not be better for you if they were looking for ways to make your life better—which is what Mr. Trump has done and will continue doing for all of us? You people need to understand that this hate they have for Mr. Trump is only because of power. They know he is doing a very good job, and it is a shame they and the media can't admit that. Mr. Trump was not a politician, ran for president, and won—and they hate him for that. This should have told everyone how fed up we are with all the empty promises and nothing being done. We need to back Mr. Trump, leave him alone, and let him do the great job he is doing.

I would like to bring up another point about the democrats. We recently lost President George Bush Sr. When Mr. Bush was in office, these Democrats treated him terribly. Now that he has passed away, they are all over TV talking how great he was just to make themselves look good. Does this show you how bad these Democrats are? My opinion on President Bush is that he was a good man and a good family man, and he did the best he could while having to deal with the Democrats. Mr. Bush and First Lady Barbara were great for this country, and my prayers are with their family.

Now I would like to talk about the upcoming third year of Mr. Trump as president. Is December 28, 2018, and in just a few days, the Democrats will take over the House. Believe me, I do not know how the hell this happened other than we had some lazy people on the Republican side run for office. We won the Senate and gained some seats, but we also had Mr. Trump doing a lot of campaigning for these seats. Can you see what is happening here? When Mr. Trump is behind people, they get elected. You Republicans need to get out there, fight for yourselves, and help us win in 2020. Anyway, the first thing we need to happen this third year is build the wall and secure our borders. The second thing is to keep taking care of our troops; they are a big part of the safety of this country. As Mr. Trump said, we need to stop fighting for all these other countries and take care of our own.

Number three, we need to get a special counsel together and investigate Hillary Clinton and everyone who was involved with her and tried to stop Donald Trump from being elected. This is very big, and if we do not do this, then we do not have equal justice in this country. Hannity and his honest team of reporters have all the facts on all of this crooked FBI and Hillary corruption. We should find the underlying cause of it and hold them all involved accountable. Again, this must be done.

Number four, we need our politicians to step up and start a campaign on a new law to put term limits on politicians so we can get rid of the ones who want to divide this country. We need people in office who want to get along. We are not always going to agree on things, but at least we can come to a compromise and make things work. There is no reason why we cannot get along, and I said it before, we need to back whoever is president, whether it is a Democrat or Republican. If America is the greatest place to be, then we need to act like it. I can only imagine what this country would be if we could get along.

Number five, we need to do something about the media and the fake news. These people should not be able to flat-out lie to the American people. The media should not be biases, but they are out of control with the way they stay on Mr. Trump and his family. It is a horrible thing to turn on the TV and see this nonsense. If they only could see how stupid they look and how bad it is for this country. We need more news like Shawn Hannity, Tucker Carlson, and Laura J. In addition, many others on Fox News take the time and tell Americans the truth.

Number six, we need to do something about the crises in our own states. The laws need to change. You know that drugs cause most of our crimes, and if we had a wall we would stop many of these drugs.

The problem with theft is that our laws are not strong enough to stop these thugs from stealing and robbing. As I mentioned earlier in this book, until we come up with laws that are strong enough to show these thieves that it is not worth it to steal, then we will always have this problem. It is a shame that every year at Christmastime, you see so much on the news about thieves stealing packages that have been delivered to people. I get so mad when I think about thieves. We talk about protecting the American people, and we need to seriously consider it because our crime rate is terrible. When I think about it, I do not think we will really know how bad our crime is until we get rid of the drugs and the illegals. I think almost everything we talk about on crime usually starts with the border. We have let this go on for so long that it is awful.

Let me change paths for a minute. I just watched Nancy Pelosi take over as speaker of the House, and it was a joke. When are any of these other Democrats going to step up and put her and Schumer in their place? It's time for one of you elected Democrats to stand up to them and stop being a chicken. Let them know your party has better people to run it. I know not all of you can be like her and Schumer; you are scared. They have made you believe if you do not think like them, then they will make life hell for you. Nancy and Schumer are not even close to being professional elected officials. They act like little kids crying to get their way. They look so ridiculous on TV, and there is nothing about them that should allow them to hold their positions. Your party would do so much better if you would get them out of there. Your party and the Republican Party need leaders who want to work together for the people and this country. I admit I do not like all the Republican officials either, but at least they try to work together and get things done.

We do have one elected senator who seems to want to be a problem, and that is Mitt Romney. I believe that the party will not put up with it. We know Mr. Trump will not take any crap from him, and Romney needs to get his head on straight and work with this party. I think he is making these comments because he is probably going to run for president in 2020. Why is it that these people who want to run for something do not talk about what they are going to do for you? All they want to do with their time is talk bad and put down whomever they are going to run against. It is just like the Democrats: all you hear from them is how they want to stop all the good things that are being done for this country, and they want to stop it because they have nothing to do with the good things that are happening.

Mr. Trump just addressed the nation on the border wall and had experts there to show and tell the American people how bad the situation is. I appreciate the fact that he takes the time to show America the truth. We all know the border has been a problem for years, but we have not had anyone who would do anything about it until now. Thank God that we have a president who is going to do something about it.

You stupid Democrats know Mr. Trump is right about this wall, and you are against it only because you cannot get over him beating you in the election. It is a shame that there are people like Schumer and Pelosi in office because they hurt this country.

Americans should want to feel safe and should want a leader that wants them to be safe. After Mr. Trump gave his speech on the border, Schumer and Pelosi had to get on TV. I could not believe how stupid they looked. I thought I was watching *The Beverly Hillbillies*. I also cannot believe you Democrats do not do something yourself about Schumer and Pelosi. You have to know they are killing your party. This is so out of control right now, and I wonder what the hell is going to happen if someone does not step in and stop all of the hate.

Now that the Democrats have taken control of the House, all you are going to see is investigation after investigation. In addition, all you are going to see them do is try to impeach the president. Is this really what you Democrats elected these politicians to do for you? I do not think so. Do you people know that those like Schumer and Pelosi live behind walls so they can feel safe? They do not care about you or the citizens who have been killed.

Another sad thing is the media and how they mislead the people who listen to their news. I will flip through channels just to see how stupid they sound. I mean, who owns these companies and allows this kind of fake news? I am watching Hannity right now, and he is at the border with President Trump and many border officers. He asked the officers if the wall would work, and they all said yes. How do you go against this? These Democrats are all about politics, and it is a damned shame. From what I hear, about three hundred Americans die each day from drugs, and we know these drugs come across our borders. This should be enough to want to build this wall. This has gone too far. Every American should see that the Democrats care only about power. They do not give a damn about our safety, only their own. We have to do something about securing our borders. It will make this country safer for our kids, and it is the duty of the president and elected officials to make the American citizens safe and make this a great country. Mr. Trump is trying very hard to make this happen. This is the future of America.

I only hope that once he gets our borders secure, he will then get with the leaders of the states and begin doing something about crime in each state. We should change our laws to make criminals think twice before they commit a crime, steal something, or even kill someone. I've said it before, but as a victim, there is nothing I hate more than a thief, and there are a lot of thefts that go on in this country. It seems like now the president has pretty good backing from the Republican Party. Thank you, Lindsey Graham, for the toughness you have brought to this party; we need more people like you who fight for what is right. The president is lucky to have you on his side.

I ask myself again, "Why can't we just get along?" I am beginning to see the Democrats have the wrong leaders in Pelosi and Schumer, and as long as they are in office, then nothing is going to change. The Republicans have to stick together and keep fighting for what is right for this country. I believe that eventually most Americans will see the right way. How can they not? Everything the president is fighting for is for us, the American people. It is like the tariffs that the president has put on these other countries that have screwed us for years. It is working. It has taken a little time, which is just like the president said, but it's all working. We are getting back our respect. You see the media and Democrats saying false things about tariffs, but it is only because they cannot take credit for what is happening. The president is doing everything he said he would do, and the Democrats cannot stand it.

Trump is the first president I know of who is standing up for America and putting America first. Again, why would everyone not be happy about this? We can see it is working, and he knew it would because he is a businessperson. If Mr. Trump had not gotten elected when he did, things would have gotten so bad for this country because we know Hillary would have not done any of this for this country. Just think about it for a minute, and it's very scary. I thank God every day that we have someone like Mr. Trump in office.

Last night on the Hannity show, he had all these parents on who had lost members of their family due to illegal immigrants. Several of them said they had been trying to get Pelosi to speak to them and look them in the eye, but she refused. This shows you how bad they are and how they are only for themselves. They want protection, but I believe they could care less for your safety. I am telling you this again and will give you a list of a few people you need to watch so you can hear the truth yourself. These are the ones I believe work hard to get the truth to US citizens: Sean Hannity, Laura Ingraham, Tucker Carlson, Mark Levin, Rush Limbaugh. They are your best choices, but there are many more. Watch Fox News, and you will get the truth and hear the facts.

I wonder what is up with that? Did they finally come to their senses? Let us hope so and thank God that he is behind us. Thank you, Colin Kaeperneck, and I'm sorry you do not have a job playing football. Well, anyways, we had a big snowfall last night, and it looks like I'm stuck at home. It's giving me a chance to write more. Remember this is the first book I've ever written, and it will probably be the only one I write. This writing is not easy, takes a lot of time, and gives me a different perspective on how much goes into writing a book.

Anyway, let us talk a little about the next two years until we get to the 2020 elections. The Democrats are going to spend all their time trying to impeach Mr. Trump because it is the only way they have a chance to take back the presidency, and they know it. They also know that Mr. Trump is doing one hell of a job, and they cannot stand it. Mr. Trump is making them look bad. The Republican party needs to start looking at the 2024 election for a candidate who has the guts that

Mr. Trump has. We are going to need someone in there who can keep everything Mr. Trump has done going forward. If you watch the fake news channels, for the next two years you are going to hear nothing but how bad Mr. Trump is and how we need to investigate everything. I have decided this year to stay only with Fox News and not flip to other channels to see and hear how stupid they sound and look.

I know it's going to be a tough time for Mr. Trump to deal with these Democrats and the fake news, but he is tough, and I believe he will get through it. You Republicans and elected officials have to stay together, back this president, and stay the course. He is on the right track to make America great again, and we must help him all the way. Remember that this is also for the future and for our children. It is the job of politicians today to make the future better for future generations. At this time, we need to forget about these damn Democrats and focus on the border wall and the economy, keeping America going on the path it is already taking. Thanks to Mr. Trump, this great country is finally heading in the right direction.

I would like to take a minute to talk about the jobs just in my town right now. I spoke earlier about this, but now we are starting Mr. Trump's third year. We are in January, when some jobs slow down. We have nearly every business in this town hiring or trying to hire people right now. Our biggest employer in town still has 170 job openings. My sister is a manager there and says they don't know what they are going to do. They are currently renovating a new building that, when done, will need additional five hundred people to start operations. There are help wanted signs up everywhere.

I want to make a point about why we need people to come here legally. If there are this many jobs in just my area alone, I can only imagine how many jobs there are across the United States. If these people want a better life, than come here legally, and they can have that better life because we have the jobs for them. My other point is we need them here—we just want them to come here legally.

America is a great place to be, and the world knows this. If we can get this wall built with things going right at the border, I believe it will be a lot easier and faster for someone to come here legal. I will say it again: I just do not understand. We are all Americans and should want each other to do well and get along. It is so sad to watch the Democrats show so much hate and want so much trouble for this country. We can only hope that something will happen to change all of that.

Now, let's think about this for a minute. I've been in the construction business for thirty years, and I've never seen so much work out there. It looks like the country is heading in the right direction, and more Americans are working than ever before.

So why not start right now, say, "Okay, we are behind this president," and let us see how good things can really get with Mr. Trump's ideas? So far it has been good. Right now as I am writing, I have the news on, and I'm hearing how supposedly the president worked for Putin and the Russians. So this is where the Democrats are going to start their crap at the beginning of this year. I believe it is going to be a crazy next two years dealing with all this fake news and made-up lies from these crazy Democrats. I know one thing: it is going to be very hard to get through these next two years until the 2020 elections. We'll have to hear all these false accusations against Mr. Trump. Remember that Democrats are going to spend their time doing things other than working for you and America. This is what you Democrats voted for, and I cannot wait until 2020 to see you people lose big.

We now have to hear the fake news media spend two more years of putting this president down. That means two more years of watching Fox News defend the president and tell the people the truth. Now, wouldn't it be nice if we could only hear about how good our economy is and how great our country is doing? Why would we not we all want this?

I feel bad for the people not being paid right now during this partial government shutdown, but I also believe they will be taken care of.

This is all so stupid and uncalled for. I am sixty-five years old, and I think back on the past years as far back as I can remember. It is amazing how much things have changed. Let us talk about just a few of the things that have changed. How many of you remember the pay phone?

They used to be everywhere. Then came the pager, and boy, did you think you were something when you had one of those clipped to your belt. You would get a page, and off you'd go to find a pay phone. Now we all carry phones that can do almost anything. For shopping, we are losing some of my favorite stores due to the way we shop now. You can turn on a computer or cell phone that has an Internet connection, order anything you want, and have it shipped right to you or to your favorite local retail store. I am already missing K-Mart and Sears. These stores have been around as long as I can remember. I guess you just have to adjust to the new way of life.

I went to look for a new Ford F-150, and they were sixty thousand dollars. I could not believe it. You used to be able to buy a house for that! Now an average house is three hundred thousand. Speaking of houses, the market is crazy right now. The houses around this area are selling for more than the asking price, new homes are being built everywhere, and the cost of a lot is averaging thirty-five to forty thousand—and double that in some locations. The problem I see with this is they call this a seller's market right now, but we all know these markets change and go through their periods. I'm afraid it will take a couple more years before the market switches again and become a buyer's market. The people who paid these high prices right now are going to lose big time. It cannot stay the way it is right now because most Americans cannot afford it. Let us see what happens but I think I am right.

I think the Fed saw this, and this is why they raised the interest rates: to try to slow down these high prices people are getting out of these homes. You have to keep it a level playing field and stop it from getting so lopsided. The economy is really booming right now, and we want to keep it that way, but we shouldn't let it get out of control. I looked into building a spec home this year for resale, but I have decided that it would have too much money on a lot that it would make it very hard to make any money. Remember, these markets always change— and you never know when it's going to happen.

This should be one crazy year to watch, with all that is going on in this country. Today, they started the drilling of Mr. Trump's attorney general, and I was able to watch a couple of hours of it. Again, some of the questions the Democrats ask are unbelievable. How mean and hateful they can treat someone? Well, I hope he gets in, and I hope he can get a special investigation going into Hillary and the FBI for all their wrongdoings. We will see. One thing that needs to happen is we need to get rid of the bias; everyone, Democrat and Republican, needs to be treated the same. We seem to keep cleaning up the FBI, and we know there are many good people. There are just the few at the top, and we have gotten rid of several of them already. This country has got to be fair and equal for everyone. We all need to believe that. Once we get the border walls up and the border secure, this will put a big hit into the drugs and crime, and then we can focus on our own bad people here in this country who want to cause trouble, commit crimes, and steal. This can easily be the greatest place in the world.

I want you to imagine having leaders at the top of both parties who would want to get along, make decisions together, and work together. This would be the greatest thing that could ever happen to this country. Imagine what could be done and accomplished!

It looks like Mr. Barr is going to be confirmed for attorney general. The questioning ended today, and we had a few Democrats and Republicans get together with Mr. Trump at the White House. It sounds like they made some progress on the government shutdown and border wall. Now, make a note to yourself that Pelosi and Schumer were not there. This is why I say if Democrats would get rid of these types of people, the two parties could work together. Today has proven that. I truly believe this will all work out. The president simply has to stay strong with his beliefs.

Now Pelosi has canceled the State of the Union address. To me, this is just another unbelievable thing that the crazy woman has done. What does she think she is doing by asking this of him? This speech is important for the American people, and I personally look forward to it every time. It just goes to show you that this woman is going to do anything to disrupt this country. All this is an attempt to stop Mr. Trump from telling America how great this country is doing and everything he has accomplished so far. She can't stand it.

The address is also important for the world to hear. They need to know where America stands and how the United States is the leader of the world. Have you seen what I think is one of the funniest things an American has done? It was done as it should have been done, and that was to stop Pelosi from using a US plane to go see the troops when we have a shutdown going on and she is unwilling to do anything to help. I would bet you that most of the troops didn't want to see her anyway; we should run a poll on that. Pelosi and Schumer have to go in order to have two parties that can get together and make decisions. As a taxpaying citizen of the United States, I want to see this political bullshit stop. I want to see what you politicians can do for us the people of the United States. This is why we have a free America and free speech. When we vote someone into office, we do this so that they will work for us and make good decisions for this country. We don't elect you just to fight the other party. The parties need to work together and come up with the best decision for everyone. Let me say this again, because I really believe it: if you put term limits on these politicians, then you will get rid of the bad ones, especially the leaders who are causing most of the problems. Remember that this is the only book I have ever written, and I probably repeat myself a lot, but I'm so frustrated with the Democratic party and the way they try to stop this country from being great again.

We should all be frustrated with the way the Democrats are treating the president. It's a shame. This is our president of the United States, and we should respect this and stand behind him. I was sitting here last night, watching Fox News and the Judge Jennie show, and thinking about this book. I said to myself, "I wonder if anyone will buy this book? Will anyone like this book?" Maybe this book will help some of you who voted against President Trump to ask yourself, "Did I make the wrong decision?" It is very clear that this man means what he says and does what he says. I will tell you again that we have never had this before and will probably never have this again, so while we do, we need to make the very most of it. I do not know that the next president who comes in here can come close to getting the things done that Mr. Trump is doing. I ask myself how we are going to deal with the next president, because I do not believe there is anyone who can come in here and get close to doing things this man has been able to do for this country. What I am trying to say is I do not think there is anyone who has the guts that Mr. Trump has, and it takes a lot of guts to take on these other countries the way he has. This is a rare time for this country. Thank god for Mr. Trump to want to come in here, fight for us, and put America first again. We all know the last president hurt this country and the pride of this country.

I would like to take a few minutes here and thank a few people, I would like to thank the men and women of our police forces all over America. You all have a very dangerous job protecting the public from US criminals. You shouldn't have to deal with the illegals who come into this country, and that's why we need this wall, but thank you for the great job you do. I would like to thank the men and women of our military. What would we do if we did not have you doing the dangerous and great job you do? You will be taken care of by this president, both now and after you have served this country. I would like to thank the politicians who do try to get along with the other party; this is the only way it should be, and you know who you are. You should be proud of it, and I thank you.

Now I would like to thank our teachers. It is a different generation of kids, and I know you have a tough job. Remember that you teachers are a big part of teaching today's children to get along with each other no matter their beliefs. My opinion on these school shootings that have happened is every school across America should have only one entrance, and that entrance should have a police officer there watching everyone coming into that school. They should go through a scanner just like at the airports, and this would end these shootings. I would like to thank Fox News and the media that tell the truth and take the time to research and make sure we know the truth. Shame on all of you who report fake news or make up lies. You bad people know who you are. Right now, the fake news is making something out of the "Make America Great Again" hat. Where will they go next?

Have you seen how many Democrats are announcing they are going to run for president? This shows you how messed up this party really is, and they know it. They are scared of their leaders and are afraid to stand up to them. Some of them think if they become president, they can get hold of their party. Can you remember when journalism used to mean something, and they would take pride in reporting the true news? Now, as we all can see, they do not care about the truth. They are run by the Democrats and are out to hurt this president. I cannot wait until it backfires on them. I have never seen so much made-up crap in my life. I keep asking myself why they hate someone who is doing everything he can to make this a great country. I think there are too many Americans who listen only to fake news channels because it is more of the local channels, and they really do not know about Fox News. What else could it be? We need to get Fox News out there even more and get the real news to everyone. Something needs to be done about these fake news networks. We must hold them accountable for misreporting and lying to the public. Don't they see how stupid they look? Just what they are thinking? Why would one American want to be so mean to another American? Why cannot we just get along? Why would we not want to get along? You know, it really scares me to think about what is going to happen in 2024 when Mr. Trump leaves office.

I am getting close to ending this book, and on the news tonight is Pelosi wanting Mr. Trump to not have the State of the Union address and told him he could not use the House chamber for the speech. This is as low as she can get. This even has to get to the Democratic Party. This is part of America, and we all want to hear the speech. This speech lets us know how our county is doing. The problem with Pelosi is she doesn't want America to hear the truth and how well this country is doing. Someone said on TV that Mr. Trump should hold the speech by the wall that is protecting Pelosi and her house. Why can't the Democrats see that this woman and Schumer are their problem? Anyway, Mr. Trump should do the speech wherever he likes to because we all will be watching.

I am going to hope that in the next two years, more people will see how bad the media is on this president and how bad Pelosi and Sherman are for the Democrats. I hope we get people in office on both sides who will start working together and get along.

As I start to end this book, it's been reported on the news that this

Mueller, who is running this damned investigation on Trump collusion, has arrested another former Trump worker, Roger Stone, for lying to someone. They are now going to destroy this man's life just as they have done to others. This is what I want to know: why in the hell hasn't Hillary and everyone who was in with her been arrested? We all know all the lies they have told. How in the hell is the one-sided investigation being allowed to happen? This is beyond belief. I have watched this for two years now, listening to all the facts that Hannity has presented time and time again. We still are letting this witch hunt go on and on. How is this possible? If we don't get Hillary and all those who were involved in the crooked things they did to try to stop Trump, then we don't have justice in this country. We have to do something. We, the people of this country, are going to be the way to do this. We have to speak up and get something done about those Democrats, or else they are going to destroy this country. They want open borders, and they care more about illegals than they do their own people. Can't we see that this is getting out of control? It's a damned shame to see this happening to this country.

I plead to all of you who care about our way of life. We must speak out and start electing people who are for this great country—not the people who want to make America a mess. I'm tired of turning on the news and hearing all the bad crap that is going on because of Democrats. The fake news needs to stop all the crap they are doing. Their misreporting is out of control and needs to stop. Even you new citizens who came here legally need to speak up. All of us must come together, join with our leaders who are not corrupt, get this under control. We must demand that we also see Hillary and her people all investigated the same as anyone else. If we don't do this, then we are going to lose this country. We can't have a one-sided justice system, and if we don't stand up to this corruption, we will lose our honesty and our laws that prevent this from happening.

You may ask why and how did we get to this place. I'll tell you again my opinion: you can't have career politicians. You must put term limits on these people. This will keep new ideas coming in and will get rid of the problem people. We must start on this now and not put this on the back burner like we have border security for so many years. We wouldn't have the problems we have now if we had protected our borders years ago, and now is our very best chance to do this. We must get behind Mr. Trump and get our borders secure. I'm afraid this will be our last chance, so please come to your senses. Let's do this. These Democrats like Pelosi and Schumer will do anything to stop securing the borders; we all know they are for open borders.

Mr. Trump has agreed to reopen the government for three weeks to try to get a deal on this border wall. We all know Pelosi and Schumer are going to do everything they can to make this difficult, but let's hope for the best. It seems as though there are some negotiations going on right now. I hope that some of these Democrats will do what they can and make this happen. I know they have a tough job given their leaders, but I think some of those Democrats will break away from Pelosi and Schumer and get a deal done so that Mr. Trump can secure the border and protect the American people and this country. This is a very serious problem, and we have to get this done.

Now we see that Pelosi is going to allow Mr. Trump to give the State of the Union address on February 5. What a joke for her to delay it. I can't wait to hear Mr. Trump's speech. The reactions from the Democrats should be the most pitiful thing the people will ever see. Anyway, we know from all the border patrol officers and experts that we need this wall. Thank god we have a president who will do whatever he has to in order to get this wall built. It's a damned shame he has to do so much fighting with these Democrats to get something done. Look at all the time that is being wasted. If they would just do what is right, this president could be focused on getting a lot of other important things done for this country.

Look at some of these Democrats who say they are running for president in 2020. Their ideas are crazy and will kill this country and everything Mr. Trump has done. It is scary to think about any of them running this country. I'm telling any of you reading this book to get with your friends and families to get people out there. Vote for the candidates who are going to help this country, not destroy it. We have a very good thing going for this country right now with Mr. Trump, and we need to stay on course.

I'm ready to end this book and would like to look back real quick on a few things that I feel are very important. All of us need to come together, back Mr. Trump, and keep America going on the track that Mr. Trump has it on. We need to change our laws on the scum who are stealing from us. Theft is terrible in this country, and we need to support our police officers because they are there to keep us safe; their job is not easy. We need to make sure our military is always taken care of because we know we can't do without them and the sacrifices they make for us. We need to change the laws of our politicians regarding term limits; these politicians get in there, think they have it made, and do nothing for us. If we put term limits on them, than this crap will stop and our parties will get along better. We need to do something about the fake news. They should not be bias and should not be able to lie and make up crap. They need to be held accountable. These are just a few things I feel are very important. Please remember that this book is only my opinion. I'm a regular US citizen with only a ninth-grade education, but I have run my own construction business for thirty-four years. I truly feel like this is the best chance America has ever had to be great, and we have Mr. Trump to thank for this. If there is anyone out there who doesn't agree with me, then please tell me the name of the last person who has even come close to doing what Mr. Trump has done for this country.

Thank you to all who read this. I hope it will help in some way. Why can't we just get along?

Printed in the United States
By Bookmasters